FRIEDA HUGHES
WOOROLOO

Frieda Hughes was born in London in 1960, and grew up in Devon. She has always painted, but wrote and illustrated children's books before she was able to give voice to her poetry.

After studying at St Martin's School of Art, she showed her work at group exhibitions in London before her first one-woman show in California in 1991. Since then she has shown her paintings in several solo and group exhibitions in Britain, America and Australia.

Her poems have appeared in many publications, including *The Guardian*, *London Magazine*, *The New Yorker* and *Paris Review*. She lives in London and is married to painter Laszlo Lukacs.

FRONT COVER SHOWS A DETAIL FROM:
Two Sheep by Frieda Hughes (1996)

Books by Frieda Hughes

CHILDREN'S BOOKS

Getting Rid of Edna
    (Heinemann, UK; Harper & Row, USA, 1986)
The Meal a Mile (Simon and Schuster, 1989)
Waldorf and the Sleeping Granny (Simon and Schuster, 1990)
The Thing in the Sink (Simon and Schuster, 1992)
Rent-a-Friend (Simon and Schuster, 1994)
The Tall Story (MacDonald Young Books, 1997)

POETRY

Wooroloo
    (HarperCollins, USA, 1998; Bloodaxe Books, UK, 1999)

FRIEDA HUGHES

Wooroloo

To John
with best wishes
Frieda Hughes.
8/6/02.

BLOODAXE BOOKS

ISBN: 1 85224 496 8

This edition published 1999 by
Bloodaxe Books Ltd,
P.O. Box 1SN,
Newcastle upon Tyne NE99 1SN.

First published in the USA in 1998 by HarperCollins.

Bloodaxe Books Ltd acknowledges
the financial assistance of Northern Arts.

Cover printing by J. Thomson Colour Printers Ltd, Glasgow.

Printed in Great Britain by
Cromwell Press Ltd, Trowbridge, Wiltshire.

For Daddy with love

ACKNOWLEDGEMENTS

Acknowledgements are due to the editors of the following publications in which some of these poems first appeared: *First Pressings* (Faber, 1998), *The Guardian, The Independent, Kunapipi, London Magazine, The New Yorker, Paris Review* and *Salt.*

CONTENTS

11   Wooroloo

12   Farmer

14   The Favour

16   The Face

17   The Wounding

20   Operation

22   Bird

23   Dead Cow

24   Foxes

25   Changes

26   The Shout

28   Spider

29   Hysterectomy

30   In the Shadow of Fire

31   Birdman

33   Thief

35   Romancing Ferret

37   Fish

39   Caesarian

40   Fire. 1

43   Teenager

44   Angry

46   Ghost

47   The Different Voice

49   Granny

50   Three Old Ladies

51   Frances

53   Rosa

55   Winifred

57   Kookaburra

58   Sandpit

59   Walrus

60   Damien's Other Cow
61   Giraffes
62   Wife
63   Earrings
64   Tiger
65   Beggar
66   The Hungarian
67   George
69   The Smile
70   Birds
71   Nothing
73   Readers
75   Laszlo
76   In Peace

Wooroloo

Wild oats pale as peroxide lie down among
The bottle brushes. A beaten army, bleaching.
Life bled into the earth already, and seeds awaiting,
Stiff little spiked children wanting water.

Above the creek that split apart the earth
With drunken gait and crooked pathway,
Kookaburras sit in eucalyptus. Squat and sharp-throated
They haggle maggots and branches from ring-neck parrots.

I have watched the green flourish twice, and die,
And the marsh dry. In this valley I have been hollowed out
And mended. I echo in my own emptiness like a tongue
In a bird's beak. My words are all gone.

Out of my mouth comes this dumb kookaburra laugh.
How my feathers itch.

Farmer

Slim, beautiful thing he was, like a dropped angel.
Eyes huge, set amazed in his face,
He wondered at the universe.
Strange man, tree watching.

She caught him young. Hollow vessel;
She saw his ownership of things, and wanted.
Saw his weakness early, nailed him to the floor
With an unexpected daughter.

Hooked, like a mouth-torn trout,
He was held fast by the cry and spit
Of little childhood begun so sudden, so surprised.
Mother felt her job was done.

Had used her womb like a weapon. Now her words
Beat him down, he was harvested in his own fields.
His bruises bloomed, those blue roses sank their stain
Beneath his surface, made him dumb with pain.

He learned to be silent.

In his head he hid. Green grew there,
Rocks cracked hot in the sun, his landscape
Was knitted by lizards and boulders of sheep.
She could not find him, or snap a bone

With the thought that made her child,
It became her stone. Its heaviness outweighed her.
At last she left him,
Strange man, tree watching.

The Favour

The man with the sickle
Is searching for something.
He wades fields of thick gold crop
In house-high boots that do not disturb
A sharp hair of grain,

But the little things
Hear him coming.
Rabbits freeze,
Their sad blood is oil
On his metal blade.

Still thirsty
He crossed a continent.
They were crushed in their slums,
In their fallen towers
In their earthquake.

He had to find them fast, find them first,
The old ones fought hardest
They knew him well,
Had seen his face often.
Not one of them wanted him.

Except the suicide in a back room,
Dangling impatiently
Her shoes off,
The chair fallen.
She was waiting.

It wasn't her time
So he broke the rope,
Gave her soul back,
Forced her to breathe it in
Like smoke.

But she wasn't having it,
She begged to be a sacrifice of no significance
At the end of a twist of hemp.
This time he took the too-soon spirit,
He put her in his pocket for later.

He is so rarely loved
He likes to keep those ones close.

The Face

Born blank, it was made up by children,
At school, with wax crayons
And small fingers sticky with sugar
From half-eaten chocolate.

It was scribbled on at home,
His mother's notepad. Thrown-away words
Sank pock-marks in those soft, white features,
Until he saw himself, a mass of chewed gum
And other people's pieces.
He had been added to by everyone,
Their fingerprints tattooed him.

Old enough to shave,
He took the blade and made
His own shape from his chin,
He sank his cheeks and sculpted creases in.
He made his face a famous thing
Until it was the signature
With which he built his prison.

The Wounding

Pretty woman. Had a name to match.
With eyes like polished stones
Still green from sea, she was man-made
In her father's thought and anger.
He used his words like tools,
To shape her up and make her outline.

When she was pencilled in, she found
She was a little on the thin side.
Rubbed out in places.
He was not happy with his work,
He thought maybe
He'd rather have a boy.

Not loved became the lesson, and she learned.
She changed her name and moved states.
Even plugged up the hole in her heart
Where her father had taken
His finger out,
And adopted a different religion.

Buried beneath this shiny new skin
Sat her old self. Carried inside
It was her unborn child,
Tossing like a rock in her hollow
And wanting her breath. Neglected,
It began to rot a little.

Its flavour rose among the organs and the blood
And found the voice. Now her words
Had this little-girl cry at their tail end.
An echo like a worm in her soil.
Want me! Want me!
Oh, to be wanted, she wanted that.

If her wanting were answered
By the man in her head, invented,
Piece by piece, impossibly,
Her small voices would surely silence.
But no one could get past the stitches
That held her heart in, where once her father lived.

She was followed by the stumbling,
And led by those without direction.
The inarticulate called after her,
But her man was none of these.
Those with purpose, who might have been,
Ignored her.

They owned the wisdom she wished for,
Enough to know she loved nothing.
Unrepentant, she had not seen her holes
As they did. Sharpened like scissors
She was just as cutting, with that odd note
From the child in her throat.

One of her old lovers, tried out and unfitted,
Was looking at his wife with eyes
That she wanted. If only
They could be in someone else's face.
She had felt those fingers before;
Left them hanging at the wrist-ends like windchimes.

Nothing about him had been good enough, but now
He was seen through those other eyes
And made beautiful.
Wife wore his face
As if she were his twin.
They had let each other in.

Within the shell of the woman
Who wouldn't give anything,
Not even the benefit of the doubt,
Unloved by her own adult,
Not saved at all,
She was screaming to be let out.

Operation

My head is lead, neck all bent
When I try to lift this melon,
I have no control. The stalk drags its fruit.
Sullen, he sits on the bed edge
Watching me helpless.

I am a damp moth with wings sticking to sheets,
Folded in creases – my chrysalis is split open
But a tube anchors me,
Leaking into my blood from a plastic bladder,
I am diluting.

He waits for me to connect my parts.
A leg slides to the floor, only minutes now
Until they lock the door, lock me in, leave me staring
Into the dark and seeing the needle
Sewn in to the open hole in my hand.

I hold still the medicine ball
That sags between my shoulders and sit,
Like a top-heavy hinge.
A small clown in open back gown,
Pale face and blood spots across my belly.

Each wound hole knitted with a single stitch,
Closing the small mouths of protesting flesh
In two bloody pouts. I am unhooked and escaping.
Each arm a dead albatross rooted in a shoulder blade,
Each leg a tree dragging mud and earth.

I am a monster of pieces.
My spirit watches from the corner
And follows at a distance,
Doesn't recognise its home.
I am alone.

Bird

Flip-top with brain
At the beak back.
Mouth so wide open
Houses would disappear.
Continents cringe, curl their toes
And hang on to their oceans.

Maw with a jaw as wide
As whatever enters. Small mice,
Large cats, or middle-size rats
With twisted whiskers.
Its call hallows the black
That brings silence.

And the body bears feathers
In its quiet. Its little soul sleeps,
So small in its twigs.
If it yawns, or belches,
There is a city in there,
With its lights on.

Dead Cow

Balloon-cow at roadside
Offers up her odour
To the flies that skate
The currents of her openings.

Their creature voices in her bloodied dark
Are met, and echoed in their eaten corridors.
A last breath, as her flesh
Offers up its children.

Foxes

Christmas night. The three of us,
Eating steak and salad without
A relative between us, beside us,
Or even at the end of a table
That would sit twelve, if we had chairs.

He appeared at the floor-deep window,
A sudden little red thought. Lost,
When we looked, like a name on a tongue-end,
Never certain. Ear tips like a claw hammer,
Face like a chisel, then gone.

He was back, two bits later, whippet body
Wanting steak fat. Half grown,
His small feet black as match heads,
His nose not able to let
The smell of meat alone.

His very presence begged us for a bite,
Hungry in the houselight. And there she was,
Just as motherless. His sister,
Coming for dinner,
Threading the field like a long needle.

Changes

I wore another woman once.
She arrived in a bucket of dye,
And began as a blond streak
With a blush like a carrot.

There I was, face beaten by the cold
In a cut-off winter, and a six-foot hearth
Burning paper left by the last supper:
The boyfriend, his girlfriend, her boyfriend

Eating without me.
Their chicken bones left to spit and crack
With the books and the bills and the savings certificates
Of total strangers. I was warm for two weeks.

This woman woke.
The streak had spread, her head was red,
Her face like stone. She swept up her ashes
And dressed differently.

She borrowed me awhile.
In fact, I had to take me back
When she married without me
And left me holding the husband.

It was only a very small box,
But the bottle inside poured me out
And coloured me in. I was found at last, in my own skin,
Still wearing her creases.

The Shout

Black sheep crawled from its mother's blood,
And staggered.
At first, it wasn't obvious the colour was wrong.
Didn't match.
Mother's job was done,
So they buried her.

Animal's legs found earth and rooted.
Mud upwards,
It grew and flowered, still wearing its mother's stain.
Strange stalk,
In a field of yellow flowers, found itself unmatched
And unrelated.

Earth-bound, knotted thing, tore ligaments and talon
From dirt, and moved forward.
Roots dragged and stumbling, it opened its mouth
And out of it
Like the dead echo of a stone now dropped again,
Came its mother's shout.

Did you die for me?
Was the voice in your head, that uglied you,
So loud it would drown me out?

Tulip-red, you took yourself to bed
And slept without me. Precious dream,
More than I was, took you from me.

Dead, you are made over.
Your face is painted in again,
And faultless, you walk.

Spider

Her hunger fresh,
She feels for the tendon
Where the fly is protesting,
Its stuck feet like the motor
Of a small boat
Burning out in weed.

The wire is tight,
The fly bedded in a soft blanket,
Is dead
With a goodnight kiss.

Hysterectomy

I want nothing left.
No threads stringing eggs like small beads
Across the bottom of an ice box.

No second chance will wear my face,
And cry out to be born
From another woman's belly.

No stolen child of mine will know
His blood was borrowed, and his third mother
Was a brittle thing, seen through like glass.

My disease will be stripped out
Like the rotten lining of a leather coat,
And, neatly sewn, I will end here.

In the Shadow of Fire

They are fast in their cars
For the children, or the milk
Or their mother.

The sky sickens, its breath is stained
With the endings of trees.

If it comes nowhere close, then
We are brave in the face of it.
We must not run.

The sun opens its orange mouth, aghast,
And puts its face out.

A silence falls as if the land
Listens,
For which parts are screaming.

Three houses and one man
Are dead already.

We hose down our tiles and our tin
And close our doors against
The smell of sacrifice.

Somewhere fire lives, breeds,
Walks forward.

Birdman

When he came out of the egg
He was fully formed and perfect,
Yet could not sing.

His bald cries echoed in his emptiness,
His unspoilt chamber,
Banging on his walls like kindling.

He had not felt the thistle whip,
Or heard a woman cry.
He had not seen his children leave,

Or watched his father die, slowly,
Enough to build a fire to give himself light
And own wisdom.

With each new pain he found a new pitch.
His voice rose among all the other voices
That roared in the heavens.

But he felt himself more naked now, than ever.
His own sweat blistered his skin and every kiss
Was a raw burn on his white underbelly.

He found endings left scars on his legs and ankles
Like scorch-marks, and beginnings were sad openings
To yet more finishing.

He packed himself up again.
Picked up his eggshell bit by bit
And stuck it to his hurt surface. Let the edges knit,

Until he was all done up and inside
His voice died. Better lost to him than stolen
By someone he loved.

Thief

It was years before I dug her out
From where her shadow lay, like a bloodstain
Beneath the black stones I had
Weighted her down with.

Her smile was crooked,
She had been dead awhile.

Back then, when the small child watched,
She said she was a relative. She beckoned,
A sweet promise coated the lips that kissed, like honey,
But her eyes were empty already.

When the child reached small hands
Into those holes, she found nothing
Behind the sounds the mouth made,
But the tongue flapping.

'Come live with me!' it cried,
Nostrils spread above like nose wings
As if the face would take off from its neck-end
Like a ghastly bald crow.

Seeing her mother was a shadow not hearing,
The father not found
To know his daughter was disappearing,
The child became blank, wiped clean like a pale sea stone.

Made herself as hollow as a dead tree,
Not worth having.
Her days were as lost as marbles, even her name
Had rolled between a crack in the floorboards.

She was stolen after all, and in her silence
The visitor grew dim. Uncertain. Receded like a dull fox
Just before dawn, barely left a scent behind
On door frames and bed linen, then was gone.

Romancing Ferret

Ferret coloured her fur
And pouted. The toads danced.
Their bellies bounced and their eyes
Bugged at the opportunity.

'No!' cried Ferret. 'Your slip-skin
And carbuncles will clog my coat,
Your breath is heavy in
My land-bound feathers,

My freedom should not go
To one of you. You will not do.'
Departing toads trailed their grease
And left their mud at her roadside.

Ferret cleaned herself again. This time,
Trout found her face at the river bottom
A thing of beauty. His gift
Was weed and caddis-fly. She almost drowned

So loaded was she by his generosity.
The larva still in her gullet,
She struggled for the river-bank. Matted, wet,
And uglied, she came face to face with stoat.

Stoat sneered at first. His oracle was sleeping
And his candle was out. He saw only
The weed-stuck spines of silt and clay,
And heard the crack of shell

In her throat-back when she spoke.
In his pity, he thought her pretty anyway,
And washed her off to find himself
Faced with his own kind.

Fish

What have I done?
I have given him back.

Thrown away something
That glittered for me,

Let it slip through my fingers,
It needed to breathe.

This fish never had my face
In its eye, it was always averted.

His lost dorsal fin was knocked off
On a rock, somewhere,

He felt its absence. Someone else
Was swimming with it now.

All I did was point out his bald back
Where he was left wanting.

Now he must decide
If he can wear it.

His worry is, it may not want him,
Being now an independent thing,

With its own trout attached.
And I am gone. A picture

Under skin of water, like a twin
Broken with the falling stone.

Caesarian

That's the trouble with these babies now;
They take one look at that hot, wet hole
And hear the traffic, and the screaming beyond,
Even only for a taxi, and they try
To climb right back up again.

A father adds up the cost already,
He is showing pennies and cents
To a dilated vagina and hoping
The kid can count.

With its feet on either side
Of its mother's gaping manhole
And with the nurses beckoning, the child
Is hanging on to the placenta
Pretending to grow there.

Until suddenly, the door opens.
Not the trapdoor with the head-clamps,
But the side door with the hip-hinges.
And it all begins.

Fire. 1

It missed me twice.
The first time at the Candlestick stadium
It caught me in its black rain.
Its sky was sick with trees and gagged
By walls and wooden floors and small dogs,
Swallowed whole.

The second time,
I sat under my tin roof
And heard the ashes rattle in the gutter. Made a wish
With every one, like coins in water.
Its footsteps levelled oat fields and skinned trees,
Quick as locusts, hot as branding irons.

This time it shouted.
And I was out. Furious,
Its voice burst fat beneath tree bark
And the possums froze in their little ash-pose.
Brittle bones pinned black
In their burning hollow.

Still, I didn't hear.
It was louder now. The neighbour's sheep
Were cooked in a field corner, and the chickens blackened
Beyond possessing even a beak or claw to make them birds.
The garage buckled in pain,
Its window dripped from the window frame.

Fire called again.
I was too far away to see
My studio twitch with its disease.
It began with a small red spot
That flowered in the floorboards,
Its anemone danced, and the music
Was the crack of wood applauding.

I wasn't in the audience
When fire ate the metal roof like a rice cracker.
Left only crumbs, a dead fridge and bottles
That had mated in their molten passion,
Where once there was the corner of a room
Beneath a sink.

Fire was there when I returned,
Watching from smoke-stumps, and barely satisfied.
In bare, black fields rose twisted squares
That were sheds once. And the studio
Lay perfect on its plot, a fresh dug grave
Punctured only by its own ribcage.

But the house remained.
All the fire hoses had been and gone
And left it clean. Soot ran right up
To the verandah, where fire had stood calling
And not been heard. Even the water-tank
Was fresh.

Fire saw this.
Above the tank grew a vast tree, rotten with life
And crawling things. Fire had hollowed it out.
Still it burned. Fire drew itself together
For a final shout, and the tree exploded,
Left the tank tangled in limbs and emptying its broken cup.

Fire was still laughing
Three days later when, in the dark –
Like musical notes left over from a large opera –
The last flames echoed from their stumps.
Eyes unslept and lips curling,
Still eating.

And now I treat blackened saplings
With water drippers and a plastic tube,
As if the land were some mammoth animal
On life-support for a small cat.
And the last leaves of the tallest trees
Have this new death-voice
As their bloodless shells clatter.

Teenager

Sweet face, soft like a fruit,
Walks with the body of a boy.
She wears her love-bite like a badge,
Blood-sucked skin by her jugular.
Doesn't want a scarf,
Just our admiration lor her decoration,
Where the red bloomed like poppies,
Branded her, and blackened in.

Angry

I heard your child crying.
Sleepless, it wore your face.

At the party, the tall man
Hung from his own shoulders.

His pills rattled in the two small rooms
Where his eyes lay unconscious.

Your child felt that man's hand on me,
Didn't see his touch on others.

Made me pay with its furious birth.
You nursed it half-way home

Beneath your coat in the car.
Until we stopped at the black beach

In a car park lit for no one,
Where no one played, or bought ice creams,

Where no one picked shells.
Where no one saw you unfold your daughter.

A deformed thing. Blind, handless, footless,
With a shout like a mallet-blow.

I wanted her dead. I smothered her cry
In fish dirt at the water's edge.

But when the silence fell
I saw you hadn't waited.

Instead, I found you home,
A heavy shadow on the garden wall

Leaning like an uprooted post,
Your hinges swinging, gateless.

Your loss of me had starved the child,
Her bitter voice was gone.

Her breathless body cracked behind
The shock that stilled your face.

We broke her worthless pieces between us
And buried her together.

Ghost

Lost, he came to watch me,
Wanting something.
Fearful of discovery
As if a dead man
Had anything to hide.

He touched me, like a blind man
Learning woman for the first time,
Fingerprint by fingerprint
Until he held my echo
In his hands.

He took my breath between his lips
To fill his hollow lungs,
And watched me live –
As if he could unbury
How he died.

Piece by piece he stole me
Until I had all gone.

The Different Voice

The fox chewed his thoughtful paw, gnawed
At his own toes and knew his differences.

When he opened his sharp mouth, long tongued
And lined with hard white spires, his voice rose

Like the howl of a ripped tree gasping for roots.
This was not a fox noise. The others listened.

Opened their mouths and out fell their words,
Dumb little shrunken heads, scattering like walnuts.

They were not in the same pain. Could not see the life
In dying things, enough to weep their passing.

They turned him over, heaved him sideways
With their curiousness, looking for flaws.

He was so like them in hair-coat and footprint,
But that voice, that voice made their own breath freeze

Like ice fog in the lung, hit by fear. That voice
Opened muddy holes in their burrow, where fear sat watching.

The same sound peeled back their eyelids,
Made them squint and sour.

But they did not think to let that light drive out their terror,
Instead, they blocked up those new corridors.

They rolled their friend into a corner, no longer a friend
But something against which to pull on their ignorance,

Like coats in the cold for each of those who spoke the same.
Spoke often, to ensure that constant recognition.

Ships' horns in sea mist, or sheep,
Lost and stupid in their search for children

All so alike, only their echoes could reach across the distance,
Until mouths found nipples and skeins were gathered in.

In the back, in the dark, the single fox
Glittered. They had missed his gold.

Granny

Mirror, mirror on the wall
Who is the least dead
Of us all?

You loved me not, just saw
A copy of the face
You gave birth to.

Wanted to catch it without warning,
Not like last time,
When it slipped away for burial. Defied you.

Chewed through its own ankle like a fox.
Left its foot in the trap
Like a lucky charm.

But I wouldn't have been that way.
Didn't have the mother-guilt,
Didn't need the approval.

Sought love from you,
But got spiked by bitter
Spearheads from your railings.

Wasn't going to bleed for you.
Wish I could cry,
But couldn't lie like you.

Three Old Ladies

Beaks open, magic cracks
Like eggshell in their dry throats.
Three marsh birds spit blood at their hospital sheets.

At night, their ghosts clatter,
Given life in the breath of old women. In the day they sit,
Each at their own bedside, visiting themselves over and over.

As long as death does not call
In his unbeatable, terrible voice
Their unfleshed bones may snap beneath their sugar paper.

Their lights are pinched
In the fingers of dark
That are putting them out.

They will use their last green twig
To keep that light burning,
Or it is all for nothing.

Frances

Haired like Beethoven, she would never
Have heard of him. Her cry was a heron,
Mud-stuck and staring up at the ceiling.
Her hands, each like a small, separate child,
Dropped things. I would collect them for her.

The spoon from the soup, or the tissues
When her blown nose had filled the sheeting.
Her nurse-cry was indignant. Surprised at her need.
Representatives of her state, and the only means
By which she moved from bed to chair,

From sleep to sleep. She called on their duty,
Her smell hanging like a damp flag,
And they 'didn't fucking know
The meaning of the word help.'
Every movement caused the knot

That locked her two knees together,
To drag pain from her twisted hip. Each jolt,
Another tooth pulled, each tooth
From a mouth a mile wide, too big to see each side.
I found out her real fear, when she asked for my help

Because there was a picnic, with children,
Two hours ago. Where were they now?
And this bed was the wrong one,
Which one should she sleep in?
And the tap dripped in a bathroom I could not reach.

In her sleep she woke, and could walk.
It was full of people she knew once.
Their laughter slapped the walls
Of our white room like a hand clap,
And the nurses with their soup and their pain,

And their ground-down powders,
Should have been the dream. She smiled at me,
Spoke my name. Eyes as big as the glass balls
That were her spectacles,
Before she slept again.

Rosa

She is sticks of seen-through blue
And pale yellows of skin. Texture
Like a camel's lip. She needs softening.
Rosa with the broken hip, is mending.

Beneath the blanket scrolling from the angle
Of her knees, she hides the hollow drum
That beat out forty years alone.
But for her son. Dark hair, dome-scraped

Wrapped in anorak. They had lived together
Until his wedding at forty-one.
Rosa smiles at me with her sheep's eye
And tells me how her new daughter is blind,

But is so clever she can find
Her way to the shops on the bus,
But could not have a house guest.
She excuses her son.

Two girls wheel her home.
She is to be planted with her climbing frame,
And allowed to flower. But a cold hand
Has cracked a pipe upstairs, like a glass straw.

One snap in the roof space, and a small murder.
Hungry water has unrolled the wallpaper
Like tongues, and the ceiling full of heavy juice,
Has fallen. The sofa floats.

Oranges are planets in the fireplace,
And the last of her son's books
Left in his old bedroom,
Have opened like sea anemones.

I meet her by the lift
As they wheel me from x-ray.
Her light is out. Her beak silent.
Her good eye and her bad eye stare

At a spot in front of her,
In equal quantities. In that spot
Are all her things. Her wet slippers, her chair lift,
Her Christmas biscuits and the floating oranges.

Two months, her son says,
Before her house is ready.
Those two months are a wall
Her hip might not climb.

She knows how hope taken
Could snuff out a candle like hers,
That dances in the growing dark,
In death's breath, and at night, in her own.

Days are only moments before her, she is carved like wax.
I ask what she sees in the floor,
In her stunned hours.
'My house,' she replies. 'My floating oranges.'

Winifred

Frances and Rosa watched her progress
And wished for her stick.
Winifred on her third leg.
Its black rubber boot beat out her hobble
To the neat, white toilet
Where she could pee, privately.
No nurse watching her jowled cheeks open
Above a bed pan.

Determined crab. She returned herself
To her dry mattress and lay,
Only a few minutes
Before she was gone again.
Frances and Rosa called for the commode,
Their four-footed frames
Were metal twins at each bed-end.

Winifred rose for the last time at lights out.
She was free for home tomorrow,
At ninety-six she was an escaping pigeon.
But took a wrong door and found
The nurses' bathroom. No wall bars.
Surprise crippled her as she hit the floor.
When her hip snapped, her wings were broken
And she was wheeled back to us.

Bones awry, hands twisted up like paper,
She sat with the face of a distressed dog,
Remembering she hadn't peed yet.
No one understood.
Except, that having fallen in the bathroom
She was, of course, relieved.
Her dark beads burrowed
Further beneath their white folds,

Trying to hide her efforts
Not to pool in her seat, like melting ice.

Kookaburra

So big in life, head like a chopping block
Beak like a carving knife,
His hysterical voice cracked branches, his laugh
Stripped bark from the wood-borers.

But in the twilight something got him,
So close to the house I should have heard.
He was left like a taunt, a dead bird
By an empty chicken run.

Now his dusk-stained feathers rock
In their dead grass cradle,
His bitten body is the flame
From which these moths escape.

That beak is buried in the sucked-out skull
Where eyes were lost in another mouth. His small crate,
Ant-eaten already, has ribs open like rafters
To welcome flies, and his wings rest like two open fans
        beside him.

Stripped of what made him
He is only a fraction of his noise.

Sandpit

Hollow pot, that one child
Is all you've got, and not even
With your eyes in her face.

You have been so forgiven
For the needle in your arm
And your legs open. The marks are gone, now.

But your coffee-cup friends are seeing
Your hand out, and empty,
Angry at not being answered.

There is nothing of you, so thin of love,
They can hold on to. All they see is through
The hole in your heart that waits for rain.

Its desert walls, where you live, will not flower
In your cold air. No lover will lie in that sand
To dry like a saltfish, where you have already died.

So dig a well for water,
And the animals will come.

Walrus

Walrus on the beach
Is bleaching like sea rock.
His whiskers and creases are dried in the sun.
In his waiting, his leather crumples
And his eyes swim like fish in his face.

His years ring him like neck chains,
And there I dangle.
I am his twitching albatross,
He can feel my heart beating,
Hears my breathing.

I am his horrible half-twin,
A half made thing.
I am parts of him and he mourns.
Sculpted like stone and sand-dug,
He beats the sea.

Anchored by sky-gulls and foot-bound by weed,
Watching my tides flow and ebb,
He feels my weight on his heart.
I am also
His badge of honour.

Sand tongues flicker in their liquid
And whisper about daughters.

Damien's Other Cow

Dead-headed, her withered lump
Has been separated from its stump.

Her petals have been peeled
By all those little black bodies he employed

And paid in sugar,
To secrete their young

Into her stolen vessel.
Egg-laid once, his blue sun

Calls them to its hot wire,
And kills them.

Giraffes

Heads huge, two sky ships sail the branch.

Enormous windows, black carbuncles, ink-filled
And shutters like lashes on a woman,
Weep with tree dust.

Green flags hang from one starboard,
The other, mouth empty, takes them
With a kiss like a collision.

Their faces knit whiskers,
Their extensions dance above crack-built bodies and below,
Legs dangle. Bone splints breaking for each step,

Every movement a swing of slow anchors.

Wife

Her face opens to show
Its forest. All those little seeds
Planted before, now grown.

Some flowering,
Some souring,
Some with people

Still caught in their branches.
That's where she hangs
Her husband.

She knows she has to let him go.
Caught fox with his claws clipped,
And his tail

Stapled to the trunk of an oak,
Where once he carved
Their initials. The cuts now bloom.

Lips that kiss in capitals.
Behind her left eye
Her old skin swings, dried in her woodland.

She must take it down from its tree
And put it on. She must remember how
She once wore her feathers.

Earrings

Pearled and gold, like florentines,
They were her ears. Your eyes
Read in them her history.
Even her voice
And the small corridor of her intellect.

She watched this sea of yours
Swim your face. Her jewels were blinding.
The suit had not offended you,
But those gold and cream suns
Applauded it, as if it had performed.

Your depth and breadth had seen
All this within those decorations.
You thought her thin, cracked like glass,
Until she turned to you and laughed,
And all your pieces lay broken.

Tiger

Tiger is born of tiger.
Looks like tiger.
Eats the same meat,
Does not complain
About its stripes.
The black slices on
Auburn red flashes
Like sun splitting thin
Black slate.
Does not complain
It looks the same.
It eats to become
Its father, to become
Its mother.

Beggar

His hollow bead
Rattled in his belly
And his sticks were folded.

Two dead chrysanthemums begged,
Bitter red at his wrist-ends,
As the train left and the play began.

He was still there,
Winter-struck on his stone,
When the play was done.

This time he faced us.
His cold centre shouting from his eye-pits
Louder than the voice that hid itself

In the warmth of his throat-root,
Made our last coins huge
In the palms of his flowers.

The Hungarian

The waiters at the restaurant
Wouldn't take him back;
Lost gift, with all his years away
Hanging about him like a necklace.
They were counting his beads,

And the eyes of his English lady,
Polished like glass,
And his perfect words
Made like flat round forints,
Kept since nineteen fifty-six.

His first night home
Was spilt with the wine and slow from the kitchen.
The cold soup without bread, then bread without butter,
Spread out on the table like a little war.
Their backs to the table pointed him out.

Make soup hot, so long since Budapest, he said.
Too late they wished they could return
The evening they had stolen.
It was nailed to the wall with his leaving,
Like a dead fish, dropping scales.

George

Lost in London, we dried in the sun at the curbside.
Between the French and the Germans
We would never have found
Our street-end, broken from the map
Somewhere across Piccadilly, like a snapped ankle.

Stone pillars hobbled a building,
Puddled the black and made caves,
And there he scratched,
His broom all part of his arm
And to-ing and fro-ing.

His scuttle body, thin as a mantis
Was tied to his twig, and each one
Swung the other. We called to him.
His long, thin load raised itself
Expecting to be wrong.

We could see the wide holes of each nostril
And his eyes, his eyes were huge from his dark.
He followed us into the sun, and in that light
His skin was seen to be knitted. Someone had tried
To make it fit. His face had been

Puzzled back into place after fire.
His mouth was open like a seed pod
To be in the warm.
All his sleeping flowers
Waiting to take root and blossom.

He didn't know our way. Living
With his head down, he didn't even see cars.
As we left, his face was snapped shut
Like a borrowed book, given back, and all his pages
Folded into the rucksack of his shoulders.

The Smile

The holes that filtered you before,
Like swamp dogs, open mouthed, are sleeping.
Their mud has sunk between your fault lines
And their bed
Rocks at the end of your corridor.
Meat eaten, the bones have dried.
Blood dust has settled like powder
With plaster from the ceiling,
And the tools are silent.
Your blunt end tries to find
A home in my face,
And your sun shines.

Birds

The poet as a penguin
Sat in his snow-cold, nursing
The egg his wife had left him.

There it was, born of them both,
Like it or not. Rounded in words,
And cracking open its shell for a voice.

In the blizzard,
Beaten up from the arctic flats
Were the audience.

From the glass extensions
Of their eyes, they watched
The skuas rise on the updraft,

Every snap of their beaks
Like the tick of a knitting needle,
Hitching a stitch in the wait

For a rolling head.

Nothing

Nothing is enough.

Nothing, with its insane grin
And rolling belly, swims in its blue.

Nothing is laughing,
Its buildings fall and nothing buries them.

I walk around nothing and try
To imagine it wrapped. My gift to you.

Nothing rocks in its cradle
Being born again.

But its hard green spires, its pine trees and oaks
Would tear paper. Its lights would go out.

Nothing has millions of eyes
And is blind.

The veins that score its surface,
That thread it with their silver and their stones,

Hold nothing in their net.
Nothing opens up its orifices

For the animals to drink. Their bodies
Feed it. Their breath

Is the breath I would give you when nothing
Nothing is a small planet.

Readers

Wanting to breathe life into their own dead babies
They took her dreams, collected words from one
Who did their suffering for them.

They fingered through her mental underwear
With every piece she wrote. Wanting her naked.
Wanting to know what made her.

Then tried to feather up the bird again.

The vulture with its bloody head
Inside its own belly,
Sucking up its own juice,

Working out its own shape,
Its own reason,
Its own death.

While their mothers lay in quiet graves
Squared out by those green cut pebbles
And flowers in a jam jar, they dug mine up.

Right down to the shells I scattered on her coffin.

They turned her over like meat on coals
To find the secrets of her withered thighs
And shrunken breasts.

They scooped out her eyes to see how she saw,
And bit away her tongue in tiny mouthfuls
To speak with her voice.

But each one tasted separate flesh,
Ate a different organ,
Touched other skin,

Insisted on being the one
Who knew best,
Who had the right recipe.

When she came out of the oven
They had gutted, peeled
And garnished her.

They called her theirs.

Laszlo

There were roses, first,
In my little fog-box
Where the nurse floated
With her one carnation.

His face followed, led
By a nose worth having a face for,
And his lips kissed.
The pethadine dripping into my tube

Almost took him from me. Bag-like, my belly
Gaped up at him with its stitched mouth,
Struck dumb from crotch to navel, my two halves
Trying to escape each other.

Intent, he listened to my breathing.
Then, light as dust, his hand
Rested on the row of bloody sutures
As if to make me whole.

In Peace

My lover is dead, at last.
His head in my lap, his hair
As yellow as grass. His weight
Has kept me rooted
For his creek and his green.

Only his parrots and kookaburras had speech.
In between, fires made them
Little more than fox dinner.
And my trees withered.
With them, I lost my words.

All that knee-bent, coil sprung
Taut voltage, that made my brushes work
And my paintings bright as flame,
Has become earthed in the dirt. Stuck in rock.
My sentences are the roadside crosses.

Language got small here.
Syllables and consonants fell off the plate
Like too many peas. Left
Just two or three to play with,
Over and over. I should lay flowers.

Much loved, that loneliness.
My man-in-the-cupboard.
But he had no voice. Just
A body to be buried in.
Had he not died first.